MW00561823

TO:

_____

FROM:

_____

DATE:

_____

Christian art gifts

© 2024 Christian Art Gifts, RSA
Christian Art Gifts Inc., IL, USA
Printed in Vietnam

DELIGHT YOURSELF IN THE LORD,
AND HE WILL GIVE YOU THE DESIRES OF YOUR HEART.

PSALM 37:4

THE LORD IS MY LIGHT AND MY SALVATION—
WHOM SHALL I FEAR? THE LORD IS THE STRONGHOLD OF
MY LIFE—OF WHOM SHALL I BE AFRAID?

PSALM 27:1

THE LORD HIMSELF GOES BEFORE YOU AND WILL
BE WITH YOU; HE WILL NEVER LEAVE
YOU NOR FORSAKE YOU.

DEUTERONOMY 31:8

GOD IS WORKING IN YOU, GIVING YOU THE DESIRE
AND THE POWER TO DO WHAT PLEASES HIM.

PHILIPPIANS 2:13

I CAN DO EVERYTHING THROUGH CHRIST,
WHO GIVES ME STRENGTH.

PHILIPPIANS 4:13

IF YOU WANT TO KNOW WHAT GOD WANTS YOU TO DO,
ASK HIM, AND HE WILL GLADLY TELL YOU.

JAMES 1:5

CREATE IN ME A PURE HEART, O GOD,
AND RENEW A STEADFAST SPIRIT WITHIN ME.

PSALM 51:10

IF ANYONE IS IN CHRIST, HE IS A NEW CREATION.
THE OLD HAS PASSED AWAY; BEHOLD, THE NEW HAS COME.

2 CORINTHIANS 5:17

CAST YOUR CARES ON THE LORD AND
HE WILL SUSTAIN YOU.

PSALM 55:22

THE LORD YOUR GOD IS IN YOUR MIDST, A MIGHTY ONE WHO
WILL SAVE; HE WILL REJOICE OVER YOU WITH GLADNESS;
HE WILL QUIET YOU BY HIS LOVE.

ZEPHANIAH 3:17

THE LORD IS TRUSTWORTHY IN ALL HE PROMISES
AND FAITHFUL IN ALL HE DOES.

PSALM 145:13

IN YOU, O LORD, DO I PUT MY TRUST AND CONFIDENTLY
TAKE REFUGE; LET ME NEVER BE PUT TO SHAME OR CONFUSION!

PSALM 71:1

"BE STRONG AND COURAGEOUS. . . . THE LORD YOUR
GOD WILL BE WITH YOU WHEREVER YOU GO."

JOSHUA 1:9

DEPEND ON THE LORD IN WHATEVER YOU DO,
AND YOUR PLANS WILL SUCCEED.

PROVERBS 16:3

SINCE WE HAVE BEEN JUSTIFIED THROUGH FAITH,
WE HAVE PEACE WITH GOD THROUGH OUR
LORD JESUS CHRIST.

ROMANS 5:1

THE LORD IS MY ROCK, MY FORTRESS AND MY DELIVERER;
MY GOD IS MY ROCK, IN WHOM I TAKE REFUGE.

PSALM 18:2

"IF ANYONE WOULD COME AFTER ME, LET HIM DENY
HIMSELF AND TAKE UP HIS CROSS AND FOLLOW ME."

MATTHEW 16:24

THE WORD OF THE LORD IS RIGHT AND TRUE;
HE IS FAITHFUL IN ALL HE DOES.

PSALM 33:4

THE LORD IS MY STRENGTH AND SHIELD.
I TRUST HIM WITH ALL MY HEART.

PSALM 28:7

IN HIM WE HAVE REDEMPTION THROUGH HIS BLOOD,
THE FORGIVENESS OF SINS, IN ACCORDANCE
WITH THE RICHES OF GOD'S GRACE.

EPHESIANS 1:7

I TRUST IN YOUR UNFAILING LOVE. I.WILL REJOICE BECAUSE
YOU HAVE RESCUED ME. I WILL SING TO THE LORD
BECAUSE HE IS GOOD TO ME.

PSALM 13:5-6

WALK IN THE WAY OF LOVE, JUST AS CHRIST LOVED
US AND GAVE HIMSELF UP FOR US AS A FRAGRANT
OFFERING AND SACRIFICE TO GOD.

EPHESIANS 5:2

"YOU WILL CALL ON ME AND COME AND PRAY TO ME,
AND I WILL LISTEN TO YOU. YOU WILL SEEK ME AND FIND ME
WHEN YOU SEEK ME WITH ALL YOUR HEART."

JEREMIAH 29:12-13

MY SOUL FINDS REST IN GOD;
MY SALVATION COMES FROM HIM.

PSALM 62:1

DELIGHT YOURSELF IN THE LORD,
AND HE WILL GIVE YOU THE DESIRES OF YOUR HEART.

PSALM 37:4

THE LORD IS MY LIGHT AND MY SALVATION—
WHOM SHALL I FEAR? THE LORD IS THE STRONGHOLD OF
MY LIFE—OF WHOM SHALL I BE AFRAID?

PSALM 27:1

THE LORD HIMSELF GOES BEFORE YOU AND WILL
BE WITH YOU; HE WILL NEVER LEAVE
YOU NOR FORSAKE YOU.

DEUTERONOMY 31:8

GOD IS WORKING IN YOU, GIVING YOU THE DESIRE
AND THE POWER TO DO WHAT PLEASES HIM.

PHILIPPIANS 2:13

I CAN DO EVERYTHING THROUGH CHRIST,
WHO GIVES ME STRENGTH.

PHILIPPIANS 4:13

IF YOU WANT TO KNOW WHAT GOD WANTS YOU TO DO,
ASK HIM, AND HE WILL GLADLY TELL YOU.

JAMES 1:5

CREATE IN ME A PURE HEART, O GOD,
AND RENEW A STEADFAST SPIRIT WITHIN ME.

PSALM 51:10

IF ANYONE IS IN CHRIST, HE IS A NEW CREATION.
THE OLD HAS PASSED AWAY; BEHOLD, THE NEW HAS COME.

2 CORINTHIANS 5:17

CAST YOUR CARES ON THE LORD AND
HE WILL SUSTAIN YOU.

PSALM 55:22

THE LORD YOUR GOD IS IN YOUR MIDST, A MIGHTY ONE WHO
WILL SAVE; HE WILL REJOICE OVER YOU WITH GLADNESS;
HE WILL QUIET YOU BY HIS LOVE.

ZEPHANIAH 3:17

THE LORD IS TRUSTWORTHY IN ALL HE PROMISES
AND FAITHFUL IN ALL HE DOES.

PSALM 145:13

IN YOU, O LORD, DO I PUT MY TRUST AND CONFIDENTLY
TAKE REFUGE; LET ME NEVER BE PUT TO SHAME OR CONFUSION!

PSALM 71:1

"BE STRONG AND COURAGEOUS. . . . THE LORD YOUR
GOD WILL BE WITH YOU WHEREVER YOU GO."

JOSHUA 1:9

DEPEND ON THE LORD IN WHATEVER YOU DO,
AND YOUR PLANS WILL SUCCEED.

PROVERBS 16:3

SINCE WE HAVE BEEN JUSTIFIED THROUGH FAITH,
WE HAVE PEACE WITH GOD THROUGH OUR
LORD JESUS CHRIST.

ROMANS 5:1

THE LORD IS MY ROCK, MY FORTRESS AND MY DELIVERER;
MY GOD IS MY ROCK, IN WHOM I TAKE REFUGE.

PSALM 18:2

"IF ANYONE WOULD COME AFTER ME, LET HIM DENY
HIMSELF AND TAKE UP HIS CROSS AND FOLLOW ME."

MATTHEW 16:24

THE WORD OF THE LORD IS RIGHT AND TRUE;
HE IS FAITHFUL IN ALL HE DOES.

PSALM 33:4

THE LORD IS MY STRENGTH AND SHIELD.
I TRUST HIM WITH ALL MY HEART.

PSALM 28:7

IN HIM WE HAVE REDEMPTION THROUGH HIS BLOOD,
THE FORGIVENESS OF SINS, IN ACCORDANCE
WITH THE RICHES OF GOD'S GRACE.

EPHESIANS 1:7

I TRUST IN YOUR UNFAILING LOVE. I WILL REJOICE BECAUSE
YOU HAVE RESCUED ME. I WILL SING TO THE LORD
BECAUSE HE IS GOOD TO ME.

PSALM 13:5-6

WALK IN THE WAY OF LOVE, JUST AS CHRIST LOVED
US AND GAVE HIMSELF UP FOR US AS A FRAGRANT
OFFERING AND SACRIFICE TO GOD.

EPHESIANS 5:2

"YOU WILL CALL ON ME AND COME AND PRAY TO ME,
AND I WILL LISTEN TO YOU. YOU WILL SEEK ME AND FIND ME
WHEN YOU SEEK ME WITH ALL YOUR HEART."

JEREMIAH 29:12-13

MY SOUL FINDS REST IN GOD;
MY SALVATION COMES FROM HIM.

PSALM 62:1

DELIGHT YOURSELF IN THE LORD,
AND HE WILL GIVE YOU THE DESIRES OF YOUR HEART.

PSALM 37:4

THE LORD IS MY LIGHT AND MY SALVATION—
WHOM SHALL I FEAR? THE LORD IS THE STRONGHOLD OF
MY LIFE—OF WHOM SHALL I BE AFRAID?

PSALM 27:1

THE LORD HIMSELF GOES BEFORE YOU AND WILL
BE WITH YOU; HE WILL NEVER LEAVE
YOU NOR FORSAKE YOU.

DEUTERONOMY 31:8

GOD IS WORKING IN YOU, GIVING YOU THE DESIRE
AND THE POWER TO DO WHAT PLEASES HIM.

PHILIPPIANS 2:13

I CAN DO EVERYTHING THROUGH CHRIST,
WHO GIVES ME STRENGTH.

PHILIPPIANS 4:13

IF YOU WANT TO KNOW WHAT GOD WANTS YOU TO DO,
ASK HIM, AND HE WILL GLADLY TELL YOU.

JAMES 1:5

CREATE IN ME A PURE HEART, O GOD,
AND RENEW A STEADFAST SPIRIT WITHIN ME.

PSALM 51:10

IF ANYONE IS IN CHRIST, HE IS A NEW CREATION.
THE OLD HAS PASSED AWAY; BEHOLD, THE NEW HAS COME.

2 CORINTHIANS 5:17

CAST YOUR CARES ON THE LORD AND
HE WILL SUSTAIN YOU.

PSALM 55:22

THE LORD YOUR GOD IS IN YOUR MIDST, A MIGHTY ONE WHO
WILL SAVE; HE WILL REJOICE OVER YOU WITH GLADNESS;
HE WILL QUIET YOU BY HIS LOVE.

ZEPHANIAH 3:17

THE LORD IS TRUSTWORTHY IN ALL HE PROMISES
AND FAITHFUL IN ALL HE DOES.

PSALM 145:13

IN YOU, O LORD, DO I PUT MY TRUST AND CONFIDENTLY
TAKE REFUGE; LET ME NEVER BE PUT TO SHAME OR CONFUSION!

PSALM 71:1

"BE STRONG AND COURAGEOUS. . . . THE LORD YOUR
GOD WILL BE WITH YOU WHEREVER YOU GO."

JOSHUA 1:9

DEPEND ON THE LORD IN WHATEVER YOU DO,
AND YOUR PLANS WILL SUCCEED.

PROVERBS 16:3

SINCE WE HAVE BEEN JUSTIFIED THROUGH FAITH,
WE HAVE PEACE WITH GOD THROUGH OUR
LORD JESUS CHRIST.

ROMANS 5:1

THE LORD IS MY ROCK, MY FORTRESS AND MY DELIVERER;
MY GOD IS MY ROCK, IN WHOM I TAKE REFUGE.

PSALM 18:2

"IF ANYONE WOULD COME AFTER ME, LET HIM DENY
HIMSELF AND TAKE UP HIS CROSS AND FOLLOW ME."

MATTHEW 16:24

THE WORD OF THE LORD IS RIGHT AND TRUE;
HE IS FAITHFUL IN ALL HE DOES.

PSALM 33:4

THE LORD IS MY STRENGTH AND SHIELD.
I TRUST HIM WITH ALL MY HEART.

PSALM 28:7

IN HIM WE HAVE REDEMPTION THROUGH HIS BLOOD,
THE FORGIVENESS OF SINS, IN ACCORDANCE
WITH THE RICHES OF GOD'S GRACE.

EPHESIANS 1:7

I TRUST IN YOUR UNFAILING LOVE. I WILL REJOICE BECAUSE
YOU HAVE RESCUED ME. I WILL SING TO THE LORD
BECAUSE HE IS GOOD TO ME.

PSALM 13:5-6

WALK IN THE WAY OF LOVE, JUST AS CHRIST LOVED
US AND GAVE HIMSELF UP FOR US AS A FRAGRANT
OFFERING AND SACRIFICE TO GOD.

EPHESIANS 5:2

"YOU WILL CALL ON ME AND COME AND PRAY TO ME,
AND I WILL LISTEN TO YOU. YOU WILL SEEK ME AND FIND ME
WHEN YOU SEEK ME WITH ALL YOUR HEART."

JEREMIAH 29:12-13

MY SOUL FINDS REST IN GOD;
MY SALVATION COMES FROM HIM.

PSALM 62:1

DELIGHT YOURSELF IN THE LORD,
AND HE WILL GIVE YOU THE DESIRES OF YOUR HEART.

PSALM 37:4

THE LORD IS MY LIGHT AND MY SALVATION—
WHOM SHALL I FEAR? THE LORD IS THE STRONGHOLD OF
MY LIFE—OF WHOM SHALL I BE AFRAID?

PSALM 27:1

THE LORD HIMSELF GOES BEFORE YOU AND WILL
BE WITH YOU; HE WILL NEVER LEAVE
YOU NOR FORSAKE YOU.

DEUTERONOMY 31:8

GOD IS WORKING IN YOU, GIVING YOU THE DESIRE
AND THE POWER TO DO WHAT PLEASES HIM.

PHILIPPIANS 2:13

I CAN DO EVERYTHING THROUGH CHRIST,
WHO GIVES ME STRENGTH.

PHILIPPIANS 4:13

IF YOU WANT TO KNOW WHAT GOD WANTS YOU TO DO,
ASK HIM, AND HE WILL GLADLY TELL YOU.

JAMES 1:5

CREATE IN ME A PURE HEART, O GOD,
AND RENEW A STEADFAST SPIRIT WITHIN ME.

PSALM 51:10

IF ANYONE IS IN CHRIST, HE IS A NEW CREATION.
THE OLD HAS PASSED AWAY; BEHOLD, THE NEW HAS COME.

2 CORINTHIANS 5:17

CAST YOUR CARES ON THE LORD AND
HE WILL SUSTAIN YOU.

PSALM 55:22

_____

_____

_____

_____

_____

_____

_____

_____

_____

_____

_____

_____

_____

_____

_____

_____

_____

_____

_____

_____

_____

_____

_____

THE LORD YOUR GOD IS IN YOUR MIDST, A MIGHTY ONE WHO
WILL SAVE; HE WILL REJOICE OVER YOU WITH GLADNESS;
HE WILL QUIET YOU BY HIS LOVE.

ZEPHANIAH 3:17

THE LORD IS TRUSTWORTHY IN ALL HE PROMISES
AND FAITHFUL IN ALL HE DOES.

PSALM 145:13

IN YOU, O LORD, DO I PUT MY TRUST AND CONFIDENTLY
TAKE REFUGE; LET ME NEVER BE PUT TO SHAME OR CONFUSION!

PSALM 71:1

"BE STRONG AND COURAGEOUS. . . . THE LORD YOUR
GOD WILL BE WITH YOU WHEREVER YOU GO."

JOSHUA 1:9

DEPEND ON THE LORD IN WHATEVER YOU DO,
AND YOUR PLANS WILL SUCCEED.

PROVERBS 16:3

SINCE WE HAVE BEEN JUSTIFIED THROUGH FAITH,
WE HAVE PEACE WITH GOD THROUGH OUR
LORD JESUS CHRIST.

ROMANS 5:1

THE LORD IS MY ROCK, MY FORTRESS AND MY DELIVERER;
MY GOD IS MY ROCK, IN WHOM I TAKE REFUGE.

PSALM 18:2

"IF ANYONE WOULD COME AFTER ME, LET HIM DENY
HIMSELF AND TAKE UP HIS CROSS AND FOLLOW ME."

MATTHEW 16:24

THE WORD OF THE LORD IS RIGHT AND TRUE;
HE IS FAITHFUL IN ALL HE DOES.

PSALM 33:4

THE LORD IS MY STRENGTH AND SHIELD.
I TRUST HIM WITH ALL MY HEART.

PSALM 28:7

IN HIM WE HAVE REDEMPTION THROUGH HIS BLOOD,
THE FORGIVENESS OF SINS, IN ACCORDANCE
WITH THE RICHES OF GOD'S GRACE.

EPHESIANS 1:7

I TRUST IN YOUR UNFAILING LOVE. I WILL REJOICE BECAUSE
YOU HAVE RESCUED ME. I WILL SING TO THE LORD
BECAUSE HE IS GOOD TO ME.

PSALM 13:5-6

WALK IN THE WAY OF LOVE, JUST AS CHRIST LOVED
US AND GAVE HIMSELF UP FOR US AS A FRAGRANT
OFFERING AND SACRIFICE TO GOD.

EPHESIANS 5:2

"YOU WILL CALL ON ME AND COME AND PRAY TO ME,
AND I WILL LISTEN TO YOU. YOU WILL SEEK ME AND FIND ME
WHEN YOU SEEK ME WITH ALL YOUR HEART."

JEREMIAH 29:12-13

MY SOUL FINDS REST IN GOD;
MY SALVATION COMES FROM HIM.

PSALM 62:1

DELIGHT YOURSELF IN THE LORD,
AND HE WILL GIVE YOU THE DESIRES OF YOUR HEART.

PSALM 37:4

THE LORD IS MY LIGHT AND MY SALVATION—
WHOM SHALL I FEAR? THE LORD IS THE STRONGHOLD OF
MY LIFE—OF WHOM SHALL I BE AFRAID?

PSALM 27:1

THE LORD HIMSELF GOES BEFORE YOU AND WILL
BE WITH YOU; HE WILL NEVER LEAVE
YOU NOR FORSAKE YOU.

DEUTERONOMY 31:8

GOD IS WORKING IN YOU, GIVING YOU THE DESIRE
AND THE POWER TO DO WHAT PLEASES HIM.

PHILIPPIANS 2:13

I CAN DO EVERYTHING THROUGH CHRIST,
WHO GIVES ME STRENGTH.

PHILIPPIANS 4:13

IF YOU WANT TO KNOW WHAT GOD WANTS YOU TO DO,
ASK HIM, AND HE WILL GLADLY TELL YOU.

JAMES 1:5

CREATE IN ME A PURE HEART, O GOD,
AND RENEW A STEADFAST SPIRIT WITHIN ME.

PSALM 51:10

IF ANYONE IS IN CHRIST, HE IS A NEW CREATION.
THE OLD HAS PASSED AWAY; BEHOLD, THE NEW HAS COME.

2 CORINTHIANS 5:17

CAST YOUR CARES ON THE LORD AND
HE WILL SUSTAIN YOU.

PSALM 55:22

_____
_____
_____
_____
_____
_____
_____
_____
_____
_____
_____
_____
_____
_____
_____
_____
_____
_____
_____
_____
_____
_____
_____
_____

THE LORD YOUR GOD IS IN YOUR MIDST, A MIGHTY ONE WHO
WILL SAVE; HE WILL REJOICE OVER YOU WITH GLADNESS;
HE WILL QUIET YOU BY HIS LOVE.

ZEPHANIAH 3:17

THE LORD IS TRUSTWORTHY IN ALL HE PROMISES
AND FAITHFUL IN ALL HE DOES.

PSALM 145:13

IN YOU, O LORD, DO I PUT MY TRUST AND CONFIDENTLY
TAKE REFUGE; LET ME NEVER BE PUT TO SHAME OR CONFUSION!

PSALM 71:1

"BE STRONG AND COURAGEOUS. . . . THE LORD YOUR
GOD WILL BE WITH YOU WHEREVER YOU GO."

JOSHUA 1:9

DEPEND ON THE LORD IN WHATEVER YOU DO,
AND YOUR PLANS WILL SUCCEED.

PROVERBS 16:3

SINCE WE HAVE BEEN JUSTIFIED THROUGH FAITH,
WE HAVE PEACE WITH GOD THROUGH OUR
LORD JESUS CHRIST.

ROMANS 5:1

THE LORD IS MY ROCK, MY FORTRESS AND MY DELIVERER;
MY GOD IS MY ROCK, IN WHOM I TAKE REFUGE.

PSALM 18:2

"IF ANYONE WOULD COME AFTER ME, LET HIM DENY
HIMSELF AND TAKE UP HIS CROSS AND FOLLOW ME."

MATTHEW 16:24

THE WORD OF THE LORD IS RIGHT AND TRUE;
HE IS FAITHFUL IN ALL HE DOES.

PSALM 33:4

THE LORD IS MY STRENGTH AND SHIELD.
I TRUST HIM WITH ALL MY HEART.

PSALM 28:7

IN HIM WE HAVE REDEMPTION THROUGH HIS BLOOD,
THE FORGIVENESS OF SINS, IN ACCORDANCE
WITH THE RICHES OF GOD'S GRACE.

EPHESIANS 1:7

I TRUST IN YOUR UNFAILING LOVE. I WILL REJOICE BECAUSE
YOU HAVE RESCUED ME. I WILL SING TO THE LORD
BECAUSE HE IS GOOD TO ME.

PSALM 13:5-6

WALK IN THE WAY OF LOVE, JUST AS CHRIST LOVED
US AND GAVE HIMSELF UP FOR US AS A FRAGRANT
OFFERING AND SACRIFICE TO GOD.

EPHESIANS 5:2

"YOU WILL CALL ON ME AND COME AND PRAY TO ME,
AND I WILL LISTEN TO YOU. YOU WILL SEEK ME AND FIND ME
WHEN YOU SEEK ME WITH ALL YOUR HEART."

JEREMIAH 29:12-13

MY SOUL FINDS REST IN GOD;
MY SALVATION COMES FROM HIM.

PSALM 62:1

DELIGHT YOURSELF IN THE LORD,
AND HE WILL GIVE YOU THE DESIRES OF YOUR HEART.

PSALM 37:4

THE LORD IS MY LIGHT AND MY SALVATION—
WHOM SHALL I FEAR? THE LORD IS THE STRONGHOLD OF
MY LIFE—OF WHOM SHALL I BE AFRAID?

PSALM 27:1

THE LORD HIMSELF GOES BEFORE YOU AND WILL
BE WITH YOU; HE WILL NEVER LEAVE
YOU NOR FORSAKE YOU.

DEUTERONOMY 31:8

GOD IS WORKING IN YOU, GIVING YOU THE DESIRE
AND THE POWER TO DO WHAT PLEASES HIM.

PHILIPPIANS 2:13

I CAN DO EVERYTHING THROUGH CHRIST,
WHO GIVES ME STRENGTH.

PHILIPPIANS 4:13

IF YOU WANT TO KNOW WHAT GOD WANTS YOU TO DO,
ASK HIM, AND HE WILL GLADLY TELL YOU.

JAMES 1:5

CREATE IN ME A PURE HEART, O GOD,
AND RENEW A STEADFAST SPIRIT WITHIN ME.

PSALM 51:10

IF ANYONE IS IN CHRIST, HE IS A NEW CREATION.
THE OLD HAS PASSED AWAY; BEHOLD, THE NEW HAS COME.

2 CORINTHIANS 5:17

CAST YOUR CARES ON THE LORD AND
HE WILL SUSTAIN YOU.

PSALM 55:22

THE LORD YOUR GOD IS IN YOUR MIDST, A MIGHTY ONE WHO
WILL SAVE; HE WILL REJOICE OVER YOU WITH GLADNESS;
HE WILL QUIET YOU BY HIS LOVE.

ZEPHANIAH 3:17

THE LORD IS TRUSTWORTHY IN ALL HE PROMISES
AND FAITHFUL IN ALL HE DOES.

PSALM 145:13

IN YOU, O LORD, DO I PUT MY TRUST AND CONFIDENTLY
TAKE REFUGE; LET ME NEVER BE PUT TO SHAME OR CONFUSION!

PSALM 71:1

"BE STRONG AND COURAGEOUS. . . . THE LORD YOUR
GOD WILL BE WITH YOU WHEREVER YOU GO."

JOSHUA 1:9

DEPEND ON THE LORD IN WHATEVER YOU DO,
AND YOUR PLANS WILL SUCCEED.

PROVERBS 16:3

SINCE WE HAVE BEEN JUSTIFIED THROUGH FAITH,
WE HAVE PEACE WITH GOD THROUGH OUR
LORD JESUS CHRIST.

ROMANS 5:1

THE LORD IS MY ROCK, MY FORTRESS AND MY DELIVERER;
MY GOD IS MY ROCK, IN WHOM I TAKE REFUGE.

PSALM 18:2

"IF ANYONE WOULD COME AFTER ME, LET HIM DENY
HIMSELF AND TAKE UP HIS CROSS AND FOLLOW ME."

MATTHEW 16:24

THE WORD OF THE LORD IS RIGHT AND TRUE;
HE IS FAITHFUL IN ALL HE DOES.

PSALM 33:4

THE LORD IS MY STRENGTH AND SHIELD.
I TRUST HIM WITH ALL MY HEART.

PSALM 28:7

IN HIM WE HAVE REDEMPTION THROUGH HIS BLOOD,
THE FORGIVENESS OF SINS, IN ACCORDANCE
WITH THE RICHES OF GOD'S GRACE.

EPHESIANS 1:7

I TRUST IN YOUR UNFAILING LOVE. I WILL REJOICE BECAUSE
YOU HAVE RESCUED ME. I WILL SING TO THE LORD
BECAUSE HE IS GOOD TO ME.

PSALM 13:5-6

WALK IN THE WAY OF LOVE, JUST AS CHRIST LOVED
US AND GAVE HIMSELF UP FOR US AS A FRAGRANT
OFFERING AND SACRIFICE TO GOD.

EPHESIANS 5:2

"YOU WILL CALL ON ME AND COME AND PRAY TO ME,
AND I WILL LISTEN TO YOU. YOU WILL SEEK ME AND FIND ME
WHEN YOU SEEK ME WITH ALL YOUR HEART."

JEREMIAH 29:12-13

MY SOUL FINDS REST IN GOD;
MY SALVATION COMES FROM HIM.

PSALM 62:1

DELIGHT YOURSELF IN THE LORD,
AND HE WILL GIVE YOU THE DESIRES OF YOUR HEART.

PSALM 37:4

THE LORD IS MY LIGHT AND MY SALVATION—
WHOM SHALL I FEAR? THE LORD IS THE STRONGHOLD OF
MY LIFE—OF WHOM SHALL I BE AFRAID?

PSALM 27:1

THE LORD HIMSELF GOES BEFORE YOU AND WILL
BE WITH YOU; HE WILL NEVER LEAVE
YOU NOR FORSAKE YOU.

DEUTERONOMY 31:8

GOD IS WORKING IN YOU, GIVING YOU THE DESIRE
AND THE POWER TO DO WHAT PLEASES HIM.

PHILIPPIANS 2:13

I CAN DO EVERYTHING THROUGH CHRIST,
WHO GIVES ME STRENGTH.

PHILIPPIANS 4:13

IF YOU WANT TO KNOW WHAT GOD WANTS YOU TO DO,
ASK HIM, AND HE WILL GLADLY TELL YOU.

JAMES 1:5

CREATE IN ME A PURE HEART, O GOD,
AND RENEW A STEADFAST SPIRIT WITHIN ME.

PSALM 51:10

IF ANYONE IS IN CHRIST, HE IS A NEW CREATION.
THE OLD HAS PASSED AWAY; BEHOLD, THE NEW HAS COME.

2 CORINTHIANS 5:17

CAST YOUR CARES ON THE LORD AND
HE WILL SUSTAIN YOU.

PSALM 55:22

THE LORD YOUR GOD IS IN YOUR MIDST, A MIGHTY ONE WHO
WILL SAVE; HE WILL REJOICE OVER YOU WITH GLADNESS;
HE WILL QUIET YOU BY HIS LOVE.

ZEPHANIAH 3:17

THE LORD IS TRUSTWORTHY IN ALL HE PROMISES
AND FAITHFUL IN ALL HE DOES.

PSALM 145:13

IN YOU, O LORD, DO I PUT MY TRUST AND CONFIDENTLY
TAKE REFUGE; LET ME NEVER BE PUT TO SHAME OR CONFUSION!

PSALM 71:1

"BE STRONG AND COURAGEOUS. . . . THE LORD YOUR
GOD WILL BE WITH YOU WHEREVER YOU GO."

JOSHUA 1:9

DEPEND ON THE LORD IN WHATEVER YOU DO,
AND YOUR PLANS WILL SUCCEED.

PROVERBS 16:3

SINCE WE HAVE BEEN JUSTIFIED THROUGH FAITH,
WE HAVE PEACE WITH GOD THROUGH OUR
LORD JESUS CHRIST.

ROMANS 5:1

THE LORD IS MY ROCK, MY FORTRESS AND MY DELIVERER;
MY GOD IS MY ROCK, IN WHOM I TAKE REFUGE.

PSALM 18:2

"IF ANYONE WOULD COME AFTER ME, LET HIM DENY
HIMSELF AND TAKE UP HIS CROSS AND FOLLOW ME."

MATTHEW 16:24

THE WORD OF THE LORD IS RIGHT AND TRUE;
HE IS FAITHFUL IN ALL HE DOES.

PSALM 33:4

THE LORD IS MY STRENGTH AND SHIELD.
I TRUST HIM WITH ALL MY HEART.

PSALM 28:7

IN HIM WE HAVE REDEMPTION THROUGH HIS BLOOD,
THE FORGIVENESS OF SINS, IN ACCORDANCE
WITH THE RICHES OF GOD'S GRACE.

EPHESIANS 1:7

I TRUST IN YOUR UNFAILING LOVE. I WILL REJOICE BECAUSE
YOU HAVE RESCUED ME. I WILL SING TO THE LORD
BECAUSE HE IS GOOD TO ME.

PSALM 13:5-6

WALK IN THE WAY OF LOVE, JUST AS CHRIST LOVED
US AND GAVE HIMSELF UP FOR US AS A FRAGRANT
OFFERING AND SACRIFICE TO GOD.

EPHESIANS 5:2

"YOU WILL CALL ON ME AND COME AND PRAY TO ME,
AND I WILL LISTEN TO YOU. YOU WILL SEEK ME AND FIND ME
WHEN YOU SEEK ME WITH ALL YOUR HEART."

JEREMIAH 29:12-13

MY SOUL FINDS REST IN GOD;
MY SALVATION COMES FROM HIM.

PSALM 62:1

DELIGHT YOURSELF IN THE LORD,
AND HE WILL GIVE YOU THE DESIRES OF YOUR HEART.

PSALM 37:4

THE LORD IS MY LIGHT AND MY SALVATION—
WHOM SHALL I FEAR? THE LORD IS THE STRONGHOLD OF
MY LIFE—OF WHOM SHALL I BE AFRAID?

PSALM 27:1

_____
_____
_____
_____
_____
_____
_____
_____
_____
_____
_____
_____
_____
_____
_____
_____
_____
_____
_____
_____
_____
_____
_____
_____

THE LORD HIMSELF GOES BEFORE YOU AND WILL
BE WITH YOU; HE WILL NEVER LEAVE
YOU NOR FORSAKE YOU.

DEUTERONOMY 31:8

GOD IS WORKING IN YOU, GIVING YOU THE DESIRE
AND THE POWER TO DO WHAT PLEASES HIM.

PHILIPPIANS 2:13

I CAN DO EVERYTHING THROUGH CHRIST,
WHO GIVES ME STRENGTH.

PHILIPPIANS 4:13

_____

_____

_____

_____

_____

_____

_____

_____

_____

_____

_____

_____

_____

_____

_____

_____

_____

_____

_____

_____

_____

_____

_____

IF YOU WANT TO KNOW WHAT GOD WANTS YOU TO DO,
ASK HIM, AND HE WILL GLADLY TELL YOU.

JAMES 1:5

CREATE IN ME A PURE HEART, O GOD,
AND RENEW A STEADFAST SPIRIT WITHIN ME.

PSALM 51:10

IF ANYONE IS IN CHRIST, HE IS A NEW CREATION.
THE OLD HAS PASSED AWAY; BEHOLD, THE NEW HAS COME.

2 CORINTHIANS 5:17

CAST YOUR CARES ON THE LORD AND
HE WILL SUSTAIN YOU.

PSALM 55:22

THE LORD YOUR GOD IS IN YOUR MIDST, A MIGHTY ONE WHO
WILL SAVE; HE WILL REJOICE OVER YOU WITH GLADNESS;
HE WILL QUIET YOU BY HIS LOVE.

ZEPHANIAH 3:17

THE LORD IS TRUSTWORTHY IN ALL HE PROMISES
AND FAITHFUL IN ALL HE DOES.

PSALM 145:13

IN YOU, O LORD, DO I PUT MY TRUST AND CONFIDENTLY
TAKE REFUGE; LET ME NEVER BE PUT TO SHAME OR CONFUSION!

PSALM 71:1

"BE STRONG AND COURAGEOUS. . . . THE LORD YOUR
GOD WILL BE WITH YOU WHEREVER YOU GO."

JOSHUA 1:9

DEPEND ON THE LORD IN WHATEVER YOU DO,
AND YOUR PLANS WILL SUCCEED.

PROVERBS 16:3

SINCE WE HAVE BEEN JUSTIFIED THROUGH FAITH,
WE HAVE PEACE WITH GOD THROUGH OUR
LORD JESUS CHRIST.

ROMANS 5:1

THE LORD IS MY ROCK, MY FORTRESS AND MY DELIVERER;
MY GOD IS MY ROCK, IN WHOM I TAKE REFUGE.

PSALM 18:2

"IF ANYONE WOULD COME AFTER ME, LET HIM DENY
HIMSELF AND TAKE UP HIS CROSS AND FOLLOW ME."

MATTHEW 16:24

THE WORD OF THE LORD IS RIGHT AND TRUE;
HE IS FAITHFUL IN ALL HE DOES.

PSALM 33:4

THE LORD IS MY STRENGTH AND SHIELD.
I TRUST HIM WITH ALL MY HEART.

PSALM 28:7

IN HIM WE HAVE REDEMPTION THROUGH HIS BLOOD,
THE FORGIVENESS OF SINS, IN ACCORDANCE
WITH THE RICHES OF GOD'S GRACE.

EPHESIANS 1:7

I TRUST IN YOUR UNFAILING LOVE. I WILL REJOICE BECAUSE
YOU HAVE RESCUED ME. I WILL SING TO THE LORD
BECAUSE HE IS GOOD TO ME.

PSALM 13:5-6

WALK IN THE WAY OF LOVE, JUST AS CHRIST LOVED
US AND GAVE HIMSELF UP FOR US AS A FRAGRANT
OFFERING AND SACRIFICE TO GOD.

EPHESIANS 5:2

"YOU WILL CALL ON ME AND COME AND PRAY TO ME,
AND I WILL LISTEN TO YOU. YOU WILL SEEK ME AND FIND ME
WHEN YOU SEEK ME WITH ALL YOUR HEART."

JEREMIAH 29:12-13

MY SOUL FINDS REST IN GOD;
MY SALVATION COMES FROM HIM.

PSALM 62:1